This book is dedicated to Shri Lord Venkateshwara Swamy of Tirumala and Tirupati

QUANTUM COMPUTING WITH PYTHON: FROM THEORY TO IMPLEMENTATION

LALASA MUKKU | JYOTHI THOMAS |
DIANA JEBA JINGLE

Made with ♥ on the Notion Press Platform
www.notionpress.com

Contents

Contents

Foreword

Quantum computing is a fascinating and rapidly evolving field that promises to transform the way we process information. It has the potential to revolutionize fields ranging from cryptography to drug discovery to machine learning. However, with this potential comes a steep learning curve. Quantum computing algorithms can be complex and difficult to understand, and the technology is still in its infancy.

This textbook on quantum computing algorithms is a welcome addition to the literature. It provides a comprehensive and accessible introduction to some of the most popular and frequently used quantum computing techniques, and it does so in a clear and concise manner. The book is well-organized and contains step-by-step instructions for implementing each algorithm using Python code.

What sets this textbook apart is its focus on applications. The authors have taken care to provide practical examples of how each algorithm can be used in the real world. This approach is particularly valuable for those who may be new to the field or who are struggling to make the connection between theory and practice. I am pleased to recommend this textbook on quantum computing algorithms to anyone interested in this exciting and rapidly evolving field.

Dr Radha

Associate Professor and Gynecologist,

&

V Mohan

Charted Accountant and Partner

Preface

Quantum computing is one of the most exciting and rapidly growing areas of research. It offers the potential to solve problems that are beyond the reach of classical computing and to open up new areas of scientific exploration. This textbook on quantum computing algorithms is the culmination of years of research and collaboration among a team of experts in the field. Our goal in writing this book is to provide a comprehensive and accessible introduction to the most popular and frequently used quantum computing techniques.

Each chapter is devoted to a specific algorithm, providing a detailed explanation of the underlying principles and step-by-step instructions for implementation using Python code. We have also included practical examples to demonstrate the wide-ranging impact of quantum computing in fields such as cryptography, optimization, and machine learning.

We believe that this textbook will be a valuable resource for students, researchers, and professionals who are interested in exploring the fascinating world of quantum computing. We hope that it will inspire and empower readers to continue their exploration of this exciting field and to contribute to the development of new algorithms and applications that will shape the future of computing.

Acknowledgements

Authors acknowledge CHRIST (Deemed to be University) for providing resources to conduct the study and research for this book

CHAPTER ONE

Introduction

Quantum computing, an emerging paradigm of information processing, promises to revolutionize our ability to solve complex computational problems that are intractable with classical computers. Quantum computers utilize the principles of quantum mechanics, a fundamental theory of physics, to perform calculations using quantum bits, or qubits, which can represent multiple states simultaneously, in contrast to classical bits that can only be in one of two states, 0 or 1. This quantum parallelism provides a significant advantage in certain computational tasks, such as factorization of large numbers and simulation of quantum systems, that are crucial for many scientific and technological applications, including cryptography, drug discovery, and materials science. Despite recent advances in hardware and algorithms, quantum computing is still in its infancy, and many challenges remain to be addressed, such as improving qubit coherence and scalability. Nevertheless, the potential benefits of quantum computing make it a fascinating and rapidly evolving field of research that is attracting a growing interest from academia, industry, and government.

The book starts with an introduction to the basics of quantum computing, including quantum mechanics, quantum gates, and quantum circuits. We then move on to describe the fundamental concepts of quantum algorithms, such as quantum parallelism, superposition, and entanglement. The book also covers quantum error correction and fault-tolerance, which are crucial for building large-scale quantum computers.

Each chapter of the book is dedicated to a specific quantum algorithm, providing a detailed description of the algorithm, its underlying principles, and its applications. We also discuss the theoretical and practical aspects of implementing these algorithms on quantum hardware, including the requirements for qubit coherence, gate fidelity, and measurement accuracy.

Throughout the book, we provide numerous examples and exercises to help readers understand the concepts and techniques presented. We also discuss the current state-of-the-art in quantum computing algorithms and the challenges that remain to be overcome in order to realize the full potential of quantum computing.

CHAPTER TWO

Quantum teleportation

Quantum teleportation is a fundamental concept in quantum information theory and is often cited as one of the earliest examples of quantum communication. It allows for the transfer of quantum states from one location to another without the actual transfer of a physical quantum particle. Instead, the quantum information is transferred through a shared entangled state between the two parties. In this chapter, we will introduce the quantum teleportation protocol and its implementation in Python.

Specifically, suppose one wants to send the qubit state |ψ?=α|0?+β|1?. This entails passing on information about α and β to others. There exists a theorem in quantum mechanics that states that you cannot simply make an exact copy of an unknown quantum state. This is known as the no-cloning theorem. As a result of this one can't simply generate a copy of |ψ? and give the copy to other. We can only copy classical states (not superpositions). However, by taking advantage of two classical bits and an entangled qubit pair, one can transfer her state |ψ? to the other. It is called teleportation because, at the end, the second one will have |ψ? and the first one won't anymore. To transfer a quantum bit, one must use a third party (Telamon) to send them an entangled qubit pair. Then performs some operations on their qubit, sends the results to others over a classical communication channel, and then performs some operations on his end to receive the sender's qubit. A third party, Telamon, creates an entangled pair of qubits and gives one to the receiver and one to the sender. The pair Telamon creates is a special pair called a Bell pair. In quantum circuit language, the way to create a Bell pair between two qubits is to first transfer one of them to the X-basis (|+? and |−?) using a Hadamard gate, and then to apply a CNOT gate onto the other qubit controlled by the one in the X-basis. The sender applies a CNOT gate to q1, controlled by |ψ? (the qubit first is trying to send the receiver). Then sender applies a Hadamard gate to |ψ?. Next, the sender applies a measurement to both qubits that she owns, q1 and |ψ?, and stores this result in two classical bits. Then sends these two bits to the receiver. The receiver, who already has the qubit q2, then applies the following gates depending on the state of the classical bits: 00 → Do nothing.

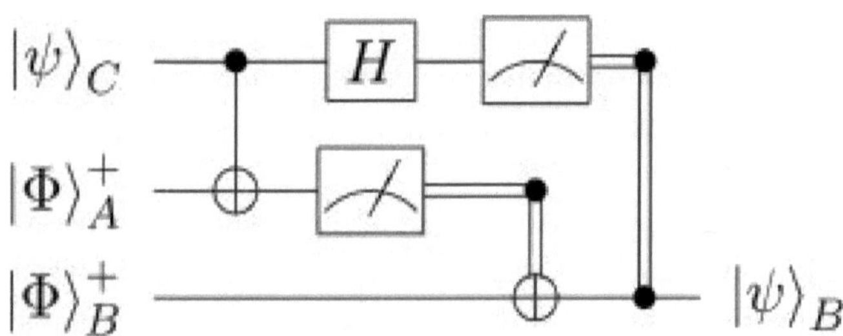

Quantum teleportation

Python code

"from qiskit import QuantumRegister, ClassicalRegister, QuantumCircuit, execute, Aer

 # Create a 3-qubit quantum register and two classical registers

q = QuantumRegister(3, 'q')

c0 = ClassicalRegister(1, 'c0')

c1 = ClassicalRegister(1, 'c1')

 # Initialize the quantum state Alice wants to send

psi = QuantumRegister(1, 'psi')

qc = QuantumCircuit(q, psi, c0, c1)

 # Apply a Hadamard gate and a CNOT gate to create the Bell pair

qc.h(q[1])

qc.cx(q[1], q[2])

 # Alice applies a CNOT gate and a Hadamard gate to the quantum state she wants to send

qc.cx(psi, q[1])

qc.h(psi)

 # Alice performs a Bell measurement on the joint state of the quantum state and her half of the entangled pair

qc.measure(q[1], c0)

qc.measure(psi, c1)

 # Bob applies a specific quantum operation to his half of the entangled pair, based on the measurement outcome he receives from Alice

qc.z(q[2]).c_if(c0, 1)

qc.x(q[2]).c_if(c1, 1)

 # Measure Bob's qubit to obtain the original state

qc.measure(q[2], 0)

```
# Execute the circuit on the qasm_simulator
backend = Aer.get_backend('qasm_simulator')
job = execute(qc, backend, shots=1)
# Get the result of the simulation
result = job.result()
print(result.get_counts())"
```

Applications

1. Quantum Cryptography: Quantum teleportation is a key component of quantum cryptography, which uses the principles of quantum mechanics to create unbreakable codes. By transmitting quantum bits (qubits) via teleportation, secure communication can be achieved.
2. Quantum Computing: Quantum teleportation is used in quantum computing as a means of transmitting quantum information between different qubits in a quantum computer. This enables the creation of more complex algorithms and computations.
3. Teleporting Quantum States: Quantum teleportation can be used to transport quantum states of atoms, molecules, and other particles from one location to another, which can have applications in fields such as quantum metrology, quantum sensing, and quantum simulation.
4. Quantum Communication: Quantum teleportation can be used to transmit quantum information across large distances, allowing for secure and high-speed communication. This has potential applications in fields such as financial transactions, military communication, and data transfer.
5. Quantum Networks: Quantum teleportation can be used as a building block for quantum networks, allowing

multiple quantum devices to communicate with each other over long distances.

In summary, quantum teleportation has the potential to revolutionize the way we communicate and compute by enabling secure and efficient transmission of quantum information.

CHAPTER THREE

Quantum phase estimation

Quantum phase estimation is a technique used to determine the phase of a unitary operator in a quantum system. It is a fundamental concept in quantum computing, with applications ranging from quantum simulation and quantum metrology to quantum algorithms for factorization and search. In classical physics, phase is a measure of the position of an oscillating system in its cycle. For example, the phase of a simple harmonic oscillator can be represented by an angle that increases linearly with time. In quantum mechanics, however, the phase of a system is more subtle, as it is not directly observable and cannot be measured directly. One way to understand the phase of a quantum system is to consider the effect of a unitary operator on the state of the system. A unitary operator is a mathematical operation that preserves the norm (length) of a state vector and the inner product between two vectors. It can be thought of as a rotation in an abstract space known as the Hilbert space. The phase of a unitary operator is a measure of the rotation it performs and can be represented by an angle. The quantum phase estimation algorithm is a method for determining the phase of a unitary operator using quantum computers. It involves preparing a special quantum state known as a superposition, applying the unitary operator multiple times, and measuring the final state. The phase can then be inferred from the measurement results using a classical computation. The quantum phase estimation algorithm has a number of important applications in quantum computing. For example, it can be used to simulate the dynamics of quantum systems, such as atoms and molecules, with greater accuracy than classical computers. It can also be used to improve the precision of measurements in quantum metrology and to speed up certain quantum algorithms such as Shor's algorithm for factorization.

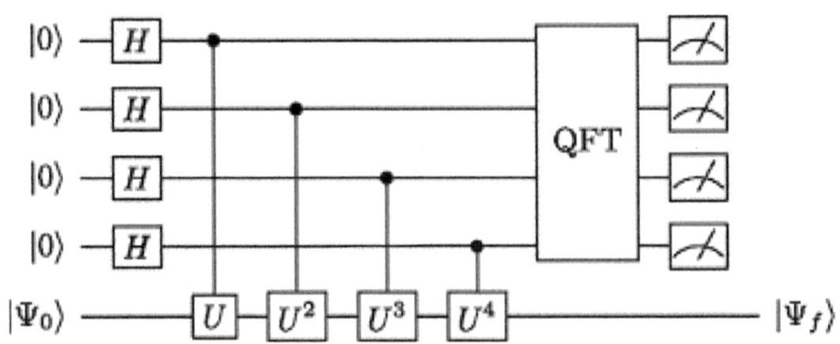

Quantum phase estimation circuit

Python code

```
"!pip install qiskit
    from qiskit import QuantumRegister,
ClassicalRegister from qiskit import
QuantumCircuit, execute,IBMQ from
qiskit.tools.monitor import job_monitor from
qiskit.circuit.library import QFT
    import numpy as np
```

```
provider = IBMQ.get_provider(hub=‘ibm-q’) backend = provider.get_backend(‘ibmq_qasm_simulator’) q = QuantumRegister(4,‘q’)
c = ClassicalRegister(3,‘c’)
circuit = QuantumCircuit(q,c)
pi = np.pi
angle = 2*(pi/3) a
actual_phase = angle/(2*pi)
#### Controlled unitary operations ####
circuit.h(q[0])
circuit.h(q[1])
circuit.h(q[2])
circuit.x(q[3])
circuit.cu1(angle, q[0], q[3]); circuit.cu1(angle, q[1], q[3]); circuit.cu1(angle, q[1], q[3]); circuit.cu1(angle, q[2], q[3]); circuit.cu1(angle, q[2], q[3]); circuit.cu1(angle, q[2], q[3]); circuit.cu1(angle, q[2], q[3]); circuit.barrier()
#### Inverse QFT ####
circuit.swap(q[0],q[2])
circuit.h(q[0])
circuit.cu1(-pi/2, q[0], q[1]);
circuit.h(q[1])
circuit.cu1(-pi/4, q[0], q[2]);
circuit.cu1(-pi/2, q[1], q[2]);
circuit.h(q[2])
circuit.barrier()
#### Measuring counting qubits #### circuit.measure(q[0],0)
circuit.measure(q[1],1)
circuit.measure(q[2],2)
```

print(circuit)

job = execute(circuit, backend, shots=8192)

job_monitor(job)

counts = job.result().get_counts()

print('\n')

print("Phase estimation output")

print("----------------------\n")

a = counts.most_frequent()

print('Most frequent measurement: ',a,'\n')

*bin_a = int(a,2) # Converts the binary value to an integer phase = bin_a/(2**3)# The calculation used to estimate the phase print('Actual phase is: ',actual_phase)*

print('Estimated phase is: ',phase)

#initialization

import matplotlib.pyplot as plt

import numpy as np

import math

 # importing Qiskit

from qiskit import IBMQ, Aer, transpile, assemble

from qiskit import QuantumCircuit, ClassicalRegister, QuantumRegister

 # import basic plot tools

from qiskit.visualization import plot_histogram

#Drawing the Circuit

qpe = QuantumCircuit(4, 3)

qpe.x(3)

for qubit in range(3):

qpe.h(qubit)

repetitions = 1

for counting_qubit in range(3):

for i in range(repetitions):

```
qpe.cp(math.pi/4, counting_qubit, 3); # This is
CU repetitions *= 2
def qft_dagger(qc, n):
for qubit in range(n//2):
qc.swap(qubit, n-qubit-1)
for j in range(n):
for m in range(j):
qc.cp(-math.pi/float(2**(j-m)), m, j)
qc.h(j)
qpe.barrier()
# Apply inverse QFT
qft_dagger(qpe, 3)
# Measure
qpe.barrier()
for n in range(3):
qpe.measure(n,n)
qpe.draw()
# Create and set up circuit
qpe3 = QuantumCircuit(6, 5)
# Apply H-Gates to counting qubits:
for qubit in range(5):
qpe3.h(qubit)
# Prepare our eigenstate |psi>:
qpe3.x(5)
# Do the controlled-U operations:
angle = 2*math.pi/3
repetitions = 1
for counting_qubit in range(5):
for i in range(repetitions):
qpe3.cp(angle, counting_qubit, 5); repetitions
*= 2
# Do the inverse QFT:
qft_dagger(qpe3, 5)
```

```
# Measure of course!
qpe3.barrier()
for n in range(5):
qpe3.measure(n,n)
aer_sim = Aer.get_backend('aer_simulator')
shots = 4096
t_qpe3 = transpile(qpe3, aer_sim)
qobj = assemble(t_qpe3, shots=shots)
results = aer_sim.run(qobj).result()
answer = results.get_counts()
plot_histogram(answer)"
```

Quantum phase estimation is performed by preparing a quantum state that is an eigenvector of the operator being estimated and then performing a series of controlled operations on the input state using the operator as the control. The controlled operations create a superposition of the input state and a second state that is related to the input state by the operator. The superposition is then measured, and the process is repeated a number of times to create a sequence of measurements.

Applications

1. Quantum simulation: One of the most promising applications of quantum computing is quantum simulation, which involves the use of quantum computers to simulate the behavior of complex systems that are difficult or impossible to simulate on classical computers. QPE can be used to efficiently determine the energy levels of a molecule, which is essential in understanding chemical reactions and designing new drugs.

2. Factoring large numbers: Shor's algorithm for factoring large numbers is one of the most well-known applications of quantum computing. QPE is a key component of Shor's algorithm, as it is used to efficiently determine the period of a modular function, which is necessary for factoring large numbers. This has important implications for cryptography, as many encryption methods rely on the difficulty of factoring large numbers.
3. Quantum machine learning: QPE has been used in quantum machine learning to estimate the eigenvalues of a Hermitian matrix, which is an essential step in many quantum algorithms for machine learning. This can be used for a variety of tasks, such as clustering and classification.
4. Optimization problems: QPE has also been used in quantum algorithms for optimization problems. For example, the quantum approximate optimization algorithm (QAOA) uses QPE to estimate the energy of a quantum state, which is used to find the optimal solution for a given optimization problem.
5. Quantum cryptography: QPE can be used to determine the phase shift between two quantum states, which is useful in quantum cryptography. This can be used to securely transmit information between two parties, as any attempt to eavesdrop on the transmission would be detectable.

CHAPTER FOUR

The Von Neumann algorithm

The von Neumann quantum algorithm, also known as the quantum iterative algorithm, is a quantum algorithm that solves linear systems of equations with exponentially fewer operations than classical algorithms. The algorithm was first proposed by John von Neumann in the 1950s as a classical iterative algorithm, but its quantum version was developed much later by Harrow, Hassidim, and Lloyd in 2009.

The basic idea of the von Neumann quantum algorithm is to use quantum phase estimation to estimate the eigenvalues of a Hermitian matrix, and then use these eigenvalues to solve the linear system of equations. The algorithm requires only logarithmic-depth quantum circuits and polynomially many queries to the matrix and its adjoint.

The algorithm proceeds as follows. Given a Hermitian matrix A and a vector b, the goal is to find a solution x to the equation Ax = b. The first step is to prepare the initial state |0?⊗n, where n is the number of qubits needed to represent the matrix A. Next, apply a series of Hadamard gates to each qubit to create a superposition of all possible basis states. This gives us the state:

|ψ? = 1/2^(n/2) Σ|j? |0?

where |j? represents the jth basis state.

Next, we use phase estimation to estimate the eigenvalues of the matrix A. This is done by applying a controlled unitary operation U = e^(2πiAt) to the state |ψ?, where t is a variable that ranges from 0 to 1. This operation effectively applies a phase shift to the state proportional to the eigenvalue of A corresponding to the eigenvector encoded by the state |j?. By varying t and applying phase estimation, we can estimate the eigenvalues of A.

Once we have estimated the eigenvalues, we can use them to solve the linear system of equations. Specifically, we can use the inverse quantum Fourier transform to map the estimated eigenvalues to solutions of the linear system. This involves applying a series of controlled rotations to the state |ψ?, followed by an inverse Fourier transform. The final state of the algorithm gives us a superposition of all solutions to the linear system, which can be measured to obtain a single solution with high probability.

In conclusion, the von Neumann quantum algorithm is a powerful quantum algorithm for solving linear systems of equations with exponential speedup over classical algorithms. It relies on quantum phase estimation to estimate the eigenvalues of a Hermitian matrix, and then uses these eigenvalues to solve the linear system. The algorithm requires only logarithmic-depth quantum circuits and polynomially many queries to the matrix and its adjoint.

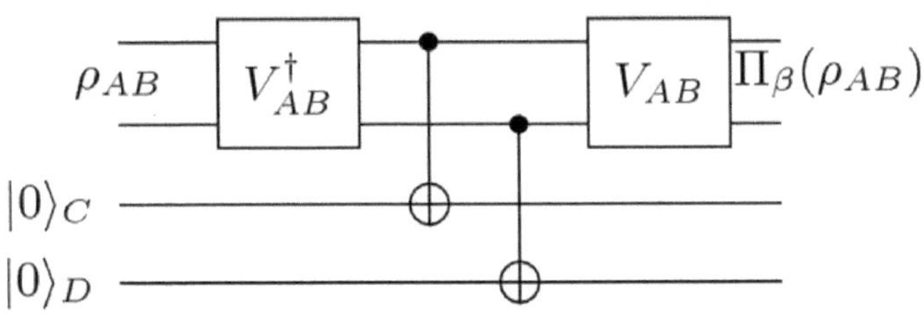

Von Neumann algorithm circuit

Python code

```
“def van_neumann(seed, num_iterations):”

# Convert seed to a string of even length by adding a zero if necessary
    seed_str = str(seed)
    if len(seed_str) % 2 == 1:
    seed_str = "0" + seed_str
    for i in range(num_iterations):
    # Square the seed and convert it to a string of even length
    squared = str(seed ** 2)
    if len(squared) % 2 == 1:
    squared = "0" + squared
    # Extract the middle digits of the squared value as the next seed
    middle_start = len(squared) // 4
    middle_end = middle_start + len(seed_str) // 2
    seed_str = squared[middle_start:middle_end]
    seed = int(seed_str)
```

 # Print the current iteration's seed value
print(seed)"

Applications

1. Integer Factorization: One of the most famous applications of Von Neumann quantum algorithms is Shor's algorithm, which is used to factor large integers. This has implications for cryptography, as many cryptographic algorithms rely on the difficulty of factoring large integers.
2. Optimization: Quantum annealing algorithms, which are a type of Von Neumann quantum algorithm, can be used to optimize problems in various fields, such as finance, logistics, and materials science.
3. Simulation: Quantum simulation algorithms can be used to simulate complex systems, such as chemical reactions and quantum systems, which are difficult to simulate with classical computers.
4. Search: Grover's algorithm is a Von Neumann quantum algorithm that can be used to speed up the process of searching an unsorted database.
5. Machine Learning: Quantum machine learning algorithms, which are based on Von Neumann quantum algorithms, can be used to perform tasks such as clustering, classification, and regression.

CHAPTER FIVE

Superdense coding

Superdense coding is a quantum algorithm that allows for the transmission of two classical bits of information by only transmitting one qubit. This algorithm is particularly useful for quantum communication protocols, where it enables the efficient exchange of information between two parties who share an entangled pair of qubits.

The superdense coding algorithm begins with a shared entangled pair of qubits in the Bell state. One of the qubits is given to Alice, and the other is given to Bob. Alice then applies one of four possible quantum gates to her qubit, depending on the two classical bits she wishes to transmit to Bob. After applying the appropriate gate, Alice sends her qubit to Bob. Bob then applies a measurement to his qubit, which yields one of four possible outcomes. Depending on the outcome, Bob can determine which two classical bits Alice wished to transmit.

To see how this works in more detail, consider the following example. Suppose Alice wishes to transmit the message "01" to Bob. Alice sends her qubit to Bob, who then applies a measurement to his qubit. If the measurement outcome is "00", Bob knows that the message must have been "00". If the outcome is "01", Bob knows that the message must have been "01". If the outcome is "10",

Bob knows that the message must have been "10". And if the outcome is "11", Bob knows that the message must have been "11". In this way, Bob can recover the two classical bits of information that Alice wished to transmit, even though she only sent him one qubit.

The superdense coding algorithm is a powerful tool in quantum communication, allowing for the efficient transmission of information between two parties who share an entangled pair of qubits. Its simplicity and elegance make it a valuable addition to the toolkit of any quantum algorithm designer or quantum communication engineer.

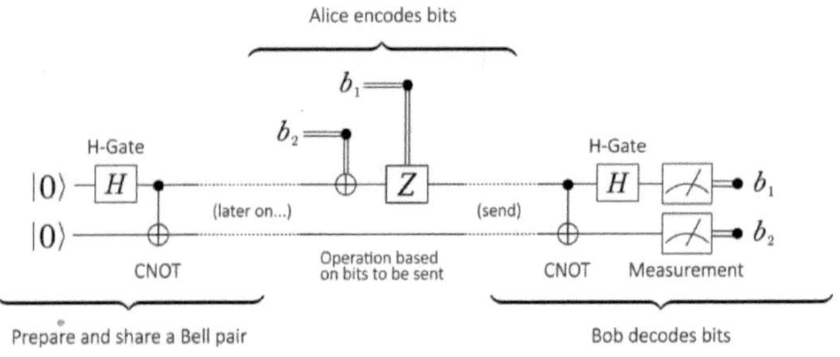

Superdense coding circuit

Python code

```
"from qiskit import QuantumCircuit, QuantumRegister, ClassicalRegister, execute, Aer
# Create a quantum circuit with 2 quantum registers and 2 classical registers
q = QuantumRegister(2, 'q')
c0 = ClassicalRegister(1, 'c0')
c1 = ClassicalRegister(1, 'c1')
```

qc = QuantumCircuit(q, c0, c1)

 # Create a Bell pair by applying a Hadamard gate to q0 and then a CNOT gate with q0 as the control and q1 as the target

qc.h(q[0])

qc.cx(q[0], q[1])

 # Alice's encoding

 # To send the message '01', Alice applies a Pauli X gate to q0, and a Pauli Z gate to q1

message = '01'

if message[0] == '1':

qc.x(q[0])

if message[1] == '1':

qc.z(q[0])

 # Bob's decoding

 # Bob applies a CNOT gate with q0 as the control and q1 as the target, followed by a Hadamard gate on q0

qc.cx(q[0], q[1])

qc.h(q[0])

 # Measure q0 and q1 and store the results in the classical registers

qc.measure(q[0], c0)

qc.measure(q[1], c1)

 # Execute the circuit on a simulator

backend = Aer.get_backend('qasm_simulator')

job = execute(qc, backend=backend, shots=1)

 # Get the result

result = job.result()

counts = result.get_counts()

 # Print the message that Bob received

print('Alice sent the message', message)

print('Bob received the message', list(counts.keys())[0])"

Applications

1. Quantum key distribution: Superdense coding can be used as a building block for quantum key distribution (QKD) protocols. In a QKD protocol, two parties (Alice and Bob) use superdense coding to share a secret key, which can then be used to encrypt and decrypt messages. Superdense coding can increase the efficiency of QKD protocols by reducing the number of qubits required to send the same amount of classical information.
2. Teleportation: Superdense coding is a key component of quantum teleportation, a protocol that allows the state of one qubit to be transferred to another qubit at a distant location. In quantum teleportation, two parties (Alice and Bob) use superdense coding to share the necessary quantum information required for teleportation.
3. Quantum computing: Superdense coding can be used in quantum computing to reduce the number of qubits required for certain computations. For example, some quantum algorithms require the distribution of classical information between different qubits. By using superdense coding, the number of qubits required for this task can be reduced.
4. Secure communication: Superdense coding can be used to send encrypted messages between two parties. By using superdense coding along with other quantum cryptographic protocols, such as quantum key distribution and quantum encryption, it is possible to

create a highly secure communication channel that is resistant to eavesdropping and other forms of attacks.

CHAPTER SIX

Shannon's noiseless channel

Shannon's noiseless channel coding theorem is a fundamental result in information theory that establishes the fundamental limits of reliable communication over a noisy channel. Specifically, the theorem states that for any given communication channel with a fixed capacity, there exists a coding scheme that allows for the transmission of information at a rate arbitrarily close to the channel capacity with negligible error probability. This result establishes the existence of a fundamental trade-off between the rate of information transmission and the probability of errors.

The proof of Shannon's noiseless channel coding theorem is based on the concept of entropy. Entropy is a measure of the randomness or uncertainty of a given random variable. In the context of information theory, entropy can be used to quantify the amount of information contained in a message or signal. Specifically, the entropy of a message is a measure of the number of bits required to represent the message in a compressed form without losing any information.

To establish the theorem, Shannon introduced the concept of a channel code, which is a mapping between the set of all possible messages and the set of all possible channel input sequences. The channel code is designed to ensure that the transmitted signal is robust against noise and can be decoded at the receiver with negligible error probability. Shannon's key insight was to use the concept of entropy to derive an upper bound on the number of distinct messages that can be reliably transmitted over a noisy channel. Specifically, he showed that the number of distinct messages that can be transmitted over a noisy channel is limited by the channel capacity, which is the maximum amount of information that can be reliably transmitted over the channel.

The proof of the theorem involves constructing a code that achieves the channel capacity and then using the entropy of the code to show that the error probability approaches zero as the code length approaches infinity. The basic idea is to use a coding scheme that assigns shorter code words to more likely messages and longer code words to less likely messages. This ensures that the probability of error decreases exponentially with the length of the code.

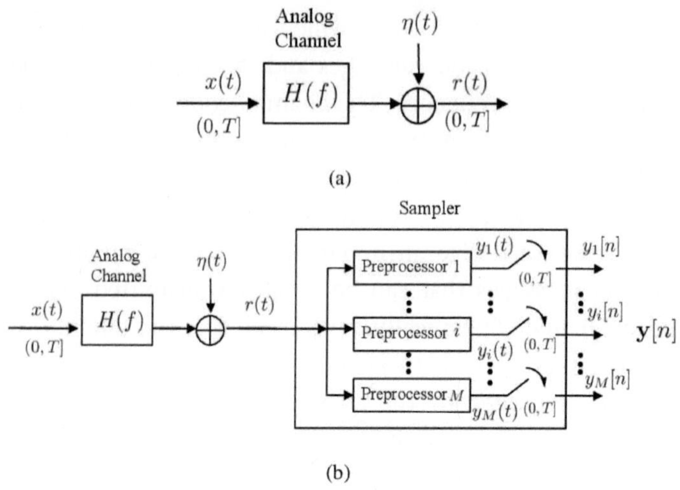

Shannon's noiseless channel circuit

Python code

```
“import math
def compute_capacity(pxy):
"""
Compute the capacity of a discrete memoryless channel with probability distribution pxy
"""
c = 0
for x, px in pxy.items():
py_given_x = pxy[x]
c += px * math.log2(py_given_x)
return c
# Example usage
channel_pxy = {‘0’: 0.9, ‘1’: 0.1}
```

 # probability of receiving 0 or 1, given 0 or 1 was sent

capacity = compute_capacity(channel_pxy)

 # compute capacity of the channel

rate = capacity / 2

 # set the rate to half the capacity (arbitrarily)

code = MyErrorCorrectingCode(rate)

 # initialize the error-correcting code

message = "Hello, world!"

encoded_message = encode_message(message, code)

 # encode the message

received_message = transmit_message(encoded_message, channel_pxy)

 # simulate transmission over the channel

decoded_message = decode_message(received_message, code)

 # decode the received message

print(decoded_message)

 # print the decoded message (should be the same as the original message)"

Applications

1. Data Compression: Shannon's theorem states that it is possible to compress data to a rate less than the channel capacity without losing any information. This concept is used in various data compression techniques such as Huffman coding, arithmetic coding, and Lempel-Ziv coding.
2. Error Correction: The theorem provides a theoretical foundation for error-correcting codes, which are widely

used to transmit data over noisy channels. Error-correcting codes are essential for reliable communication in many applications, including satellite communication, mobile communication, and internet communication.

3. Cryptography: Shannon's theorem also has applications in cryptography, where it is used to ensure the confidentiality of communication. The theorem shows that it is possible to transmit a message in such a way that an eavesdropper cannot decode it, provided the rate of transmission is less than the channel capacity.
4. Signal Processing: Shannon's theorem is also used in digital signal processing to optimize the use of communication channels. For example, it is used to design filter banks and to calculate the sampling rate required to ensure accurate signal reconstruction.

CHAPTER SEVEN

Quantum annealing

Quantum Annealing (QA) is a powerful optimization algorithm that harnesses the principles of quantum mechanics to find the global minimum of a given cost function. It has been extensively studied in the field of quantum computing, particularly in the context of adiabatic quantum computation (AQC), where the system is evolved slowly enough to ensure that it remains in its ground state throughout the evolution.

The basic idea behind QA is to map the problem to be solved onto a Hamiltonian that can be implemented on a quantum annealer, which is a specialized type of quantum computer that is designed to implement such Hamiltonians. The Hamiltonian is constructed in such a way that the ground state of the system corresponds to the solution of the problem.

To achieve this, the Hamiltonian is defined as a linear combination of two terms: the first term encodes the problem to be solved, while the second term is a simple driver Hamiltonian that can be easily implemented on the quantum annealer. The driver Hamiltonian is usually chosen to be a simple, diagonal matrix with all diagonal elements equal to one.

The system is initialized in the ground state of the driver Hamiltonian, which is a simple product state with all qubits in the |0\rangle state. The system is then evolved from the driver Hamiltonian to the problem Hamiltonian, with the evolution being controlled by a time-dependent parameter s that varies from 0 to 1. The Hamiltonian is given by:

H(s) = (1-s) H_d + s H_p

where H_d is the driver Hamiltonian and H_p is the problem Hamiltonian.

The evolution is controlled by the parameter s, which is slowly increased from 0 to 1 over a certain time period. The evolution is said to be adiabatic if it is slow enough to ensure that the system remains in its ground state throughout the evolution. At the end of the evolution, the system is measured and the result is decoded to obtain the solution to the problem.

The success of the algorithm depends on several factors, such as the choice of the problem Hamiltonian, the speed of the evolution, and the number of qubits in the system. Despite these challenges, QA has shown promising results for a variety of optimization problems, including optimization of classical spin glasses, graph partitioning, and error correction in quantum computing.

In conclusion, Quantum Annealing is a powerful optimization algorithm that utilizes the principles of quantum mechanics to find the global minimum of a given cost function. The algorithm is based on adiabatic quantum computation, where the system is evolved slowly enough to ensure that it remains in its ground state throughout the evolution. The success of the algorithm depends on several factors, such as the choice of the problem Hamiltonian, the speed of the evolution, and the number of qubits in the system. Despite these challenges, QA has shown promising results for a variety of optimization problems, making it a valuable tool in the field of quantum computing.

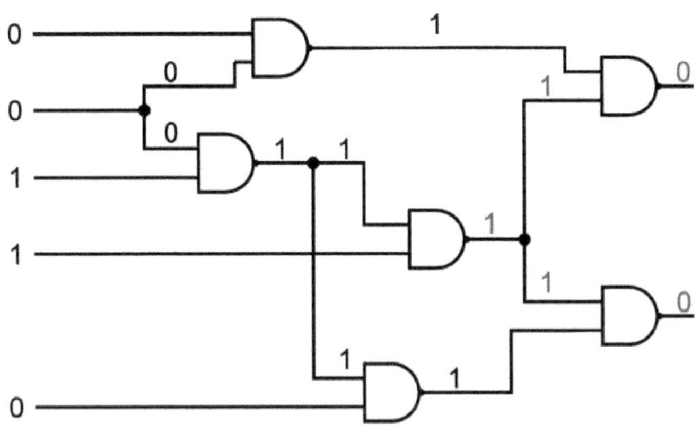

Quantum annealing circuit

Python code

```
“import dwavebinarycsp
import dwave.inspector
from dwave.system import DWaveSampler, EmbeddingComposite
# Define the Ising model
h = {0: -1, 1: 2, 2: -2} # linear biases
J = {(0, 1): -1, (1, 2): 2, (0, 2): -2} # quadratic biases
# Create a binary CSP from the Ising model
csp = dwavebinarycsp.BinaryCSP.from_ising(h, J)
# Compile the CSP for the D-Wave quantum computer
bqm = dwavebinarycsp.stitch(csp)
```

```
# Define the D-Wave solver and sampler
sampler = EmbeddingComposite(DWaveSampler())
response = sampler.sample(bqm, num_reads=1000)
# Print the results
for sample, energy in response.data(['sample', 'energy']):
print(sample, energy)
# Visualize the results using the D-Wave Inspector
dwave.inspector.show(response)"
```

Note that this code assumes that you have access to a D-Wave quantum computer and have configured your environment to work with it. The '*DWaveSampler*' class provides an interface to the D-Wave quantum computer, while the '*EmbeddingComposite*' class maps the problem to the physical qubits of the D-Wave quantum computer.

In the code above, we define a simple 'Ising' model with three variables and use '*dwavebinarycsp*' to create a binary CSP from it. We then use *stitch* to compile the CSP into a binary quadratic model (BQM) that can be solved by the D-Wave quantum computer. Finally, we use the '*DWaveSampler*' to sample the BQM and retrieve the results.

Applications

1. Optimization problems: Quantum annealing can be used to solve optimization problems, such as finding the shortest route between multiple points or finding the optimal allocation of resources.

2. Machine learning: Quantum annealing can be used to improve machine learning algorithms, such as deep learning and reinforcement learning, by solving optimization problems more efficiently.
3. Cryptography: Quantum annealing can be used to develop new cryptographic algorithms that are more secure than traditional encryption methods.
4. Financial modelling: Quantum annealing can be used to simulate financial models, such as portfolio optimization and risk management, more accurately and efficiently.
5. Drug discovery: Quantum annealing can be used to speed up the process of drug discovery by simulating the behaviour of molecules more efficiently.
6. Supply chain optimization: Quantum annealing can be used to optimize supply chain operations, such as scheduling and routing, to reduce costs and increase efficiency.
7. Traffic optimization: Quantum annealing can be used to optimize traffic flow, such as finding the best route for emergency services or reducing congestion during rush hours.

CHAPTER EIGHT

Gaussian Boson Sampling

In recent years, the Gaussian Boson Sampling problem has emerged as a promising candidate for demonstrating the computational power of quantum computers. In this problem, one aims to sample from the output distribution of a quantum circuit that consists of Gaussian operations and photon number measurements.

The output distribution of such a circuit is characterized by the so-called bosonic permanents, which are generalizations of the classical permanent to the bosonic Fock space. Computing these permanents is known to be a computationally hard problem classically, which suggests that sampling from the output distribution of a Gaussian Boson Sampling circuit should also be hard. However, despite the hardness of computing bosonic permanents, the output distribution of a Gaussian Boson Sampling circuit can be efficiently simulated classically using the so-called Gottesman-Knill theorem. This result is based on the fact that Gaussian operations can be efficiently simulated classically, and that photon number measurements can be simulated using classical probabilities.

The question then arises: why should one care about the Gaussian Boson Sampling problem if it can be efficiently simulated classically? The answer lies in the fact that Gaussian Boson Sampling is believed to be hard even for quantum computers, which makes it a potential candidate for demonstrating quantum supremacy – the idea that quantum computers can outperform classical computers on certain tasks. Moreover, Gaussian Boson Sampling has applications in areas such as molecular simulations and optimization, where sampling from the output distribution of a quantum circuit can provide valuable insights into the behaviour of complex systems.

In summary, the Gaussian Boson Sampling problem is an important problem in quantum computing that aims to sample from the output distribution of a quantum circuit consisting of Gaussian operations and photon number measurements. Despite being efficiently simulatable classically, it is believed to be hard for quantum computers, making it a potential candidate for demonstrating quantum supremacy and having practical applications in areas such as molecular simulations and optimization.

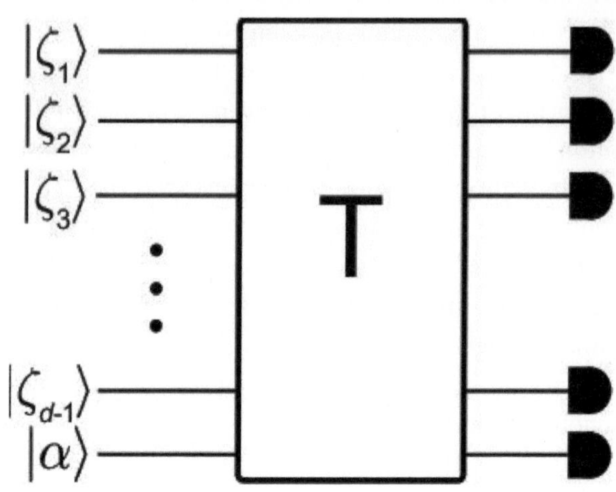

Gaussian Boson Sampling circuit

Python code

```
"import strawberryfields as sf
from strawberryfields.ops import Sgate, BSgate, MeasureX
# set the number of modes and mean photon number
num_modes = 4
mean_photon_num = 2
# initialize the quantum circuit
eng, q = sf.Engine(num_modes)
# apply Squeezing gates to each mode
for mode in range(num_modes):
Sgate(r=1) | q[mode]
# apply a beamsplitter gate between each pair of modes
for i in range(num_modes):
```

for j in range(i+1, num_modes):
BSgate() | (q[i], q[j])
 # measure the output of the circuit using the x-quadrature measurement
for mode in range(num_modes):
MeasureX() | q[mode]
 # run the circuit and collect the measurement results
*results = eng.run('gaussian', cutoff_dim=10, hbar=2*mean_photon_num).samples*
 # print the measurement results
print("Measurement results:")
for mode in range(num_modes):
print(f"Mode {mode}: {results[f'qumode[{mode}]'][‘x’]}")"

This code initializes a quantum circuit with 'num_modes' modes and applies a Squeezing gate to each mode with squeezing parameter 'r=1'. Then, it applies a beamsplitter gate between each pair of modes, and measures the output of the circuit using the x-quadrature measurement. The 'cutoff_dim' parameter specifies the size of the Fock space truncation used in the simulation, and 'hbar' is the value of Planck's constant used in the simulation. The samples method returns a dictionary of measurement results for each mode, which are printed to the console.

Applications

1. Quantum Computing: GBS is considered a promising platform for quantum computing because it is experimentally feasible and has a low error rate. It can be used to perform quantum simulations of complex systems, such as biological molecules, materials, and

chemical reactions.

2. Machine Learning: GBS has been shown to have potential applications in machine learning. It can be used to perform tasks such as pattern recognition, clustering, and classification. GBS has been demonstrated to be computationally hard, making it a potential tool for building secure and efficient machine learning algorithms.
3. Cryptography: GBS has also been proposed as a potential tool for post-quantum cryptography. It has been shown that GBS can be used to generate random numbers that are difficult to predict, making it a promising candidate for encryption and other cryptographic applications.
4. Optimization: GBS has potential applications in optimization problems, such as portfolio optimization, network optimization, and logistics optimization. It has been shown that GBS can be used to find the optimal solutions to these problems more efficiently than classical computers

CHAPTER NINE

Shor's Factor Finding Algorithm

Shor's factor finding algorithm is a quantum algorithm designed to factor large integers efficiently. It was first proposed by Peter Shor in 1994, and has since become one of the most well-known quantum algorithms due to its potential to break modern cryptographic systems. The algorithm works by leveraging the properties of quantum mechanics to perform a computation in parallel. In classical computing, the best known algorithms for factoring integers require an exponential number of operations, making them infeasible for large numbers. However, in quantum computing, the parallelism offered by quantum states allows for the computation of all possible factors simultaneously, leading to an exponential speedup in the time required to factor an integer.

Shor's algorithm begins by preparing the input state as a superposition of all possible values of the factor to be found. This is achieved through a quantum Fourier transform, which transforms the input state into a superposition of all possible values of the period of a function that is related to the factor to be found. The period of this function is then measured using a quantum measurement, which results in a random value that is a multiple of the period with high probability. Next, the algorithm uses the value obtained from the measurement to find a factor of the original integer using classical algorithms. This step is efficient because the period of the function is related to the factors of the integer through a mathematical property known as Euler's theorem.

The main challenge in implementing Shor's algorithm is the need to perform the quantum Fourier transform, which requires a large number of quantum gates and is therefore susceptible to errors. Additionally, the measurement step in the algorithm requires a large number of qubits, which is currently beyond the capabilities of most quantum computers. Despite these challenges, Shor's algorithm remains an active area of research in quantum computing due to its potential to break modern cryptographic systems. While the algorithm has not yet been demonstrated on a large scale quantum computer, advances in quantum hardware and error correction techniques suggest that this may be possible in the near future.

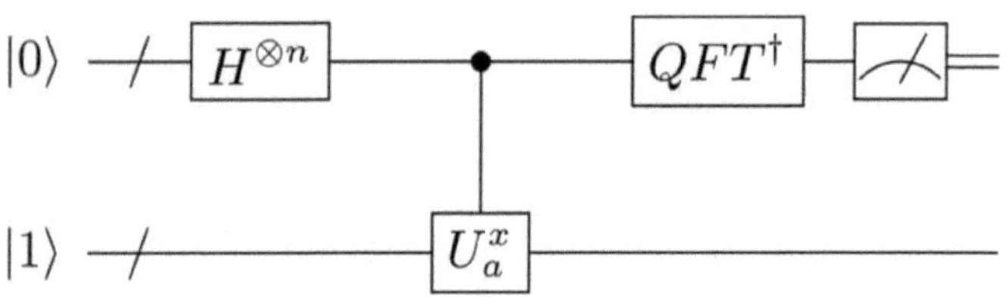

Shor's Factor Finding circuit

Python code

"*from qiskit import QuantumCircuit, Aer, execute*

from qiskit.aqua import QuantumInstance
from qiskit.aqua.algorithms import Shor
 # Define the number to be factored
N = 15
 # Set up a quantum circuit with the required number of qubits
qc = QuantumCircuit(8, 4)
 # Apply quantum gates to prepare the input state
qc.h(range(4))
 # Apply the quantum Fourier transform to create a superposition of period values
qc.append(Shor.qft(4, approximation_degree=0), range(4))
 # Measure the period
qc.measure(range(4), range(4))
 # Run the circuit on a quantum simulator
backend = Aer.get_backend('qasm_simulator')
quantum_instance = QuantumInstance(backend)
algorithm = Shor(N)
result = algorithm.run(quantum_instance)
 # Print the factorization result
print("Factors found:", result['factors'])"

Applications

1. Quantum Chemistry: Shor's algorithm can be used to simulate quantum systems. This can be used to study the structure and properties of molecules and materials, which are important for many scientific and industrial applications.

2. Machine Learning: Shor's algorithm can be used to efficiently train neural networks. This can be used to speed up the training process and improve the accuracy of machine learning models.
3. Optimization: Shor's algorithm can be applied to optimization problems, to find the optimal solutions to a given set of parameters. as RSA, which depend on the difficulty of factoring large numbers.
4. String Matching: Shor's algorithm is used in string matching algorithms, to identify and match strings of characters within a large data set.
5. Cryptography: Shor's algorithm is used in cryptography to break public key encryption such as RSA.

CHAPTER TEN

Grovers algorithm

Grover's algorithm is a quantum algorithm that provides a quadratic speedup over classical algorithms for unstructured search problems. The algorithm aims to find a marked element in an unsorted database of N elements with a success probability close to unity using O(sqrt(N)) queries to the database. The algorithm's working involves three main components: a quantum state preparation step, a quantum query, and a quantum amplitude amplification procedure. In the state preparation step, a uniform superposition of all possible states is created using a quantum Fourier transform on N qubits. This state serves as the input to the algorithm.

The quantum query step implements an oracle function that marks the solution states by inverting their amplitudes, while keeping the other states unchanged. The oracle function can be implemented using a classical circuit or a black box unitary operation. In the amplitude amplification step, the algorithm iteratively applies a sequence of two operations, called the diffusion operator and the oracle operator, to the initial superposition state. The diffusion operator reflects the amplitudes around the mean amplitude of the superposition, while the oracle operator inverts the amplitudes of the marked states. This sequence of operations amplifies the amplitudes of the marked states and suppresses the amplitudes of the unmarked states, resulting in a higher probability of measuring a marked state.

The number of iterations required to achieve a high success probability depends on the number of marked states and the size of the database. It can be shown that the optimal number of iterations is proportional to sqrt(N/M), where M is the number of marked states. Grover's algorithm has several applications in computer science and cryptography, including database search, element distinctness, and graph theory. It also serves as a building block for other quantum algorithms, such as Shor's algorithm for factorization and discrete logarithms. Despite its theoretical advantages, practical implementations of Grover's algorithm face several challenges, including the need for fault-tolerant quantum hardware and the high error rates in quantum gates and measurements.

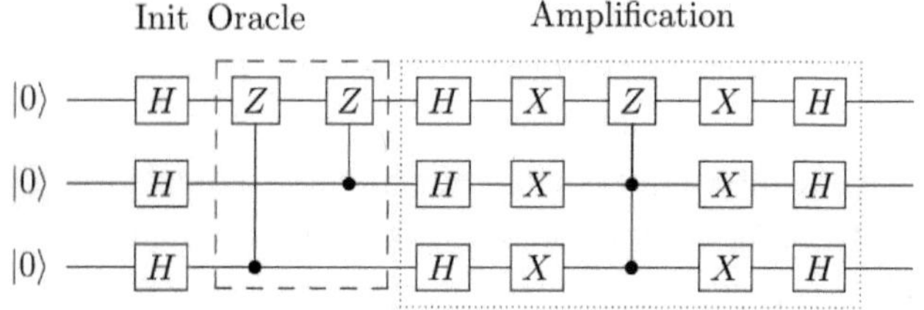

Grovers algorithm circuit

Python code

```
"import numpy as np
  # Define the Oracle function
```

```
def oracle(x, target):
if x == target:
return 1
else:
return -1
# Define the Diffusion Operator
def diffusion_operator(n):
H = np.identity(2**n) - 2 * np.ones((2**n, 2**n)) / (2**n)
return H
# Define Grover's Algorithm
def grovers_algorithm(n, target):
# Initialize variables
N = 2**n
iterations = int(np.pi/4*np.sqrt(N))
state = np.ones(N) / np.sqrt(N)
# Apply Grover's Algorithm
for i in range(iterations):
# Apply the Oracle
for j in range(N):
state[j] *= oracle(j, target)
# Apply the Diffusion Operator
state = diffusion_operator(n).dot(state)
# Return the Result
return np.argmax(state)
# Example Usage
n = 3
target = 6
result = grovers_algorithm(n, target)
print("The target value is:", target)
print("The result of Grover's Algorithm is:", result)”
```

Applications

1. Database search: Grover's algorithm can be used to search an unsorted database in O(sqrt(N)) time, where N is the number of items in the database. This can be useful in various fields like data analysis, image processing, and scientific research.
2. Optimization: Grover's algorithm can be used as a subroutine in optimization algorithms, such as the Quantum Approximate Optimization Algorithm (QAOA), to find the optimal solution faster than classical methods.
3. Cryptography: Grover's algorithm can be used to break symmetric cryptographic systems, such as AES encryption, by searching for the key in O(sqrt(N)) time. This has implications for post-quantum cryptography and the development of quantum-safe cryptography.
4. Machine learning: Grover's algorithm can be used in certain machine learning applications, such as training quantum neural networks and clustering large datasets.
5. Graph theory: Grover's algorithm can be used to find the minimum spanning tree of a graph, which has applications in transportation networks, electrical grids, and social networks.

CHAPTER ELEVEN

Simon Algorithm

The Simon algorithm, named after its inventor Daniel Simon, is a prime example of a quantum algorithm that exhibits exponential speedup over its classical counterpart. The algorithm aims to solve the so-called "hidden subgroup problem", which involves finding a hidden subgroup of a given group. At its core, the Simon algorithm works by exploiting the properties of entanglement and interference in a quantum system. More specifically, the algorithm uses a quantum circuit that takes as input a superposition of all possible values of the hidden subgroup and then applies a sequence of quantum gates to this input state.

The key insight behind the Simon algorithm is that the output of this quantum circuit, when measured, will reveal information about the hidden subgroup. In particular, if the output of the quantum circuit is entangled, then the algorithm can efficiently determine the structure of the hidden subgroup by performing a series of measurements and exploiting the resulting correlations. This quantum approach to the hidden subgroup problem provides a dramatic improvement over classical algorithms, which require an exponential number of queries to the function defining the hidden subgroup in order to obtain the same information. In contrast, the Simon algorithm only requires a polynomial number of quantum operations to achieve the same result, leading to a significant speedup in the computation time.

Overall, the Simon algorithm provides a powerful demonstration of the potential of quantum computing to tackle complex computational problems that are beyond the reach of classical computers. While still in its infancy, the field of quantum computing promises to revolutionize many areas of science and technology, and the Simon algorithm serves as a powerful example of the kinds of breakthroughs that are possible in this exciting new field.

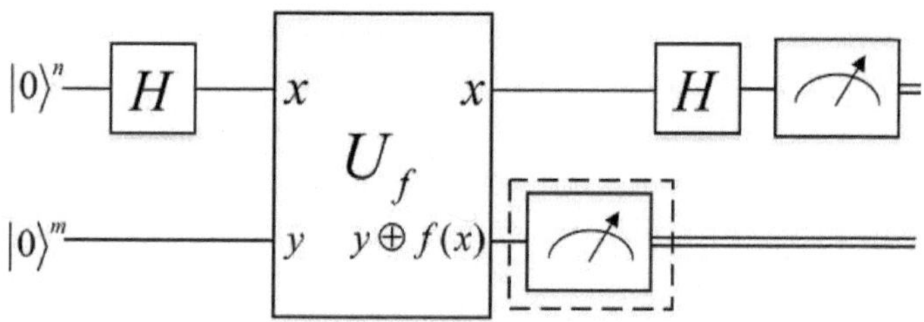

Simon algorithm circuit

Python code

```
“from qiskit import QuantumCircuit, Aer, execute
from qiskit.quantum_info import Statevector
import numpy as np
def simon_algorithm(oracle):
# Determine the size of the input and output registers
n = len(list(oracle.keys())[0])
m = len(list(oracle.values())[0])
# Create the quantum circuit
```

```
qc = QuantumCircuit(n + m, n)
# Apply Hadamard gates to the input register
for i in range(n):
qc.h(i)
# Apply the oracle function to the circuit
for x, fx in oracle.items():
for i in range(n):
if x[i] == ‘1’:
qc.cx(i, n + int(fx, 2))
# Apply Hadamard gates to the input register again
for i in range(n):
qc.h(i)
# Measure the input register
for i in range(n):
qc.measure(i, i)
# Simulate the circuit and get the measurement outcomes
backend = Aer.get_backend(‘qasm_simulator’)
counts = execute(qc, backend).result().get_counts()
# Determine the period from the measurement outcomes
for x, count in counts.items():
if count > 1:
period = np.bitwise_xor(int(x), int(list(counts.keys())[0]))
return format(period, ‘0’ + str(n) + ‘b’)”
```

Applications

1. Cryptography: The Simon algorithm can be used to break classical cryptographic schemes that rely on the

difficulty of finding the period of a function. For example, it can be used to break the RSA cryptosystem, which is widely used in modern cryptography.

2. Optimization: The Simon algorithm can be used to speed up certain optimization algorithms. For example, it can be used to solve the shortest vector problem, which is a fundamental problem in lattice-based cryptography and optimization.
3. Chemistry: The Simon algorithm can be used to simulate molecular systems, which is important in the field of quantum chemistry. By finding the period of a function that describes the behaviour of a molecule, researchers can gain insight into its properties and behaviour.
4. Machine Learning: The Simon algorithm can be used to speed up certain machine learning algorithms. For example, it can be used to solve the linear systems of equations that arise in support vector machine algorithms.
5. Coding theory: The Simon algorithm can be used to construct error-correcting codes, which are used to protect data transmitted over noisy channels. By finding the period of a function, researchers can construct codes with better error-correcting properties.

CHAPTER TWELVE

Quantum Counting algorithm

The Quantum Counting algorithm is a powerful quantum algorithm that provides exponential speedup over its classical counterpart for a wide range of counting problems. This algorithm is based on the principles of quantum phase estimation and amplitude amplification, two important concepts in quantum computing that allow for efficient quantum algorithms for a wide range of problems.

The Quantum Counting algorithm works by encoding the solution to a counting problem as a phase shift in a quantum state. Specifically, the algorithm uses a unitary operator that maps the input state to a state where the solution to the counting problem is encoded as a phase shift. The quantum phase estimation algorithm is then applied to this state, allowing for the extraction of the phase shift with high probability.

To amplify the amplitude of the phase shift, the algorithm uses the technique of amplitude amplification. This involves applying a sequence of two unitary operators that act as a quantum version of a binary search. This amplifies the amplitude of the phase shift by a factor of the square root of the number of solutions to the counting problem.

Overall, the Quantum Counting algorithm provides a significant speedup over classical algorithms for a wide range of counting problems, including problems in computer science, combinatorics, and graph theory. It is a powerful demonstration of the potential of quantum computing to solve complex problems that are beyond the reach of classical computers.

However, the Quantum Counting algorithm is not without its limitations. It requires access to an oracle that can evaluate the function being counted, and it is sensitive to errors in the phase estimation and amplitude amplification steps. Additionally, it requires a large number of quantum gates and qubits, making it challenging to implement in practice.

Despite these challenges, the Quantum Counting algorithm remains an important tool in the quantum computing toolbox, and its development represents a significant step forward in our understanding of the power and potential of quantum computing.

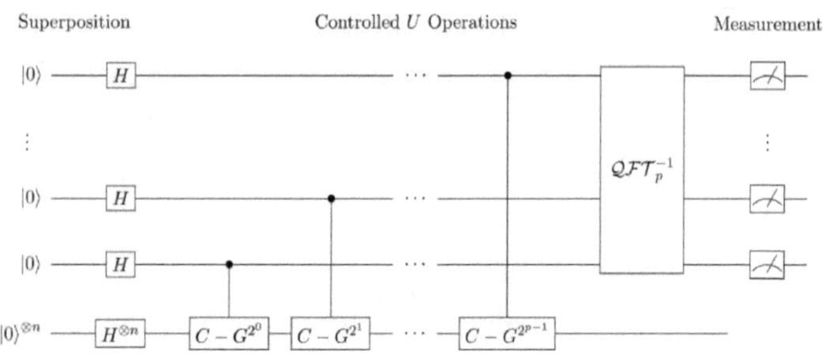

Quantum counting algorithm circuit

Python code

```
"import math
from qiskit import Aer, execute, QuantumCircuit
from qiskit.quantum_info import Statevector
# Define the Quantum Counting Function
def quantum_counting(n, U):
# Create quantum circuit with n+1 qubits and n classical bits
qc = QuantumCircuit(n+1, n)
qc.h(range(n))
qc.x(n)
qc.h(n)
# Apply U gate
qc.append(U, list(range(n+1)))
# Apply inverse quantum Fourier transform
for i in range(n):
qc.h(i)
for j in range(i+1, n):
qc.cu1(-2*math.pi/2**(j-i+1), j, i)
qc.barrier()
# Measure first n qubits
qc.measure(range(n), range(n))
# Execute circuit on a simulator
backend = Aer.get_backend('qasm_simulator')
result = execute(qc, backend, shots=1024).result()
counts = result.get_counts()
# Calculate the estimated value of the number of solutions
s = sum([int(k) * v for k,v in counts.items()])
m = 1024
```

*theta = 2*math.asin(math.sqrt(s/m))*
N = math.ceil(math.pi/2/theta)
return N"

Applications

1. Computational Biology: The Quantum Counting algorithm has significant applications in computational biology, particularly in analyzing large datasets of DNA sequences. It can be used to estimate the number of distinct DNA sequences in a sample, which is critical for understanding the diversity of microbial communities, identifying novel species, and tracking the evolution of viruses.
2. Data Analysis: The Quantum Counting algorithm has important applications in data analysis and database search. It can be used to estimate the number of unique IP addresses in a network, the number of users who have interacted with a particular website, or the number of matches for a particular query in a database. This has important implications for search engines, social media analytics, and recommendation systems.
3. Machine Learning: The Quantum Counting algorithm has implications for quantum machine learning, where it can be used to estimate the number of data points in a dataset, the number of clusters in a clustering algorithm, or the number of parameters in a quantum neural network. This has the potential to improve the efficiency and accuracy of quantum machine learning algorithms, which are critical for a wide range of applications, including finance, drug discovery, and materials science.

4. Cryptography: The Quantum Counting algorithm can also be used in cryptography, particularly in the construction of quantum-resistant cryptographic protocols. The algorithm can be used to estimate the number of solutions to a Boolean formula or the number of occurrences of a particular pattern in a string, which are key building blocks for several cryptographic protocols.

CHAPTER THIRTEEN

Deutsch-Josza

The Deutsch-Josza algorithm, proposed by David Deutsch and Richard Josza in 1992, is one of the earliest quantum computing algorithms that demonstrated the power of quantum computing in solving a classically hard problem. The algorithm aims to determine whether a given black-box function is constant or balanced with only one query to the function, where constant means that the function returns the same value for all inputs, and balanced means that the function returns two different values equally often.

To understand the working of the Deutsch-Josza algorithm, let us consider a black-box function f that takes an n-bit string as input and returns either 0 or 1. In the classical case, we need to query the function at least 2^(n-1) + 1 times to determine whether it is constant or balanced, which is exponentially many queries for large n. However, the Deutsch-Josza algorithm provides a quantum speed-up by using a quantum circuit that consists of n qubits and a single ancillary qubit.

The algorithm proceeds as follows. First, we prepare n qubits in the state |0?^n and the ancillary qubit in the state |1?. Next, we apply a Hadamard gate to each qubit, which puts the qubits in a superposition of all possible n-bit strings. The resulting state is (|0? + |1?)^n ⊗ |1? / sqrt(2^(n+1)). Then, we apply the black-box function f to the n qubits, controlled by the ancillary qubit, which maps the state to (|0?^n ⊗ |f(0)⊕1? + |1?^n ⊗ |f(1)⊕1?) / sqrt(2^(n+1))). Finally, we apply a Hadamard gate to each qubit except the ancillary qubit, which results in the state:

((-1)^f(0) / sqrt(2^(n+1))) * (|0?^n ⊗ |0?) +
((-1)^f(1) / sqrt(2^(n+1))) * (|0?^n ⊗ |1?) +
((-1)^f(2) / sqrt(2^(n+1))) * (|1?^n ⊗ |0?) +
((-1)^f(3) / sqrt(2^(n+1))) * (|1?^n ⊗ |1?) +

where the coefficients of the terms depend on the values of f. If f is constant, then all coefficients have the same sign, and the state collapses to either |0?^n ⊗ |0? or |1?^n ⊗ |1? with probability 1. If f is balanced, then the coefficients of the terms with an even number of qubits in the |1? state cancel out, and the state collapses to a superposition of |0?^n ⊗ |1? and |1?^n ⊗ |0? with probability 1/2 each.

Thus, by measuring the ancillary qubit, we can determine whether f is constant or balanced with only one query to the function, which is a quadratic speed-up over the classical case. The Deutsch-Josza algorithm illustrates the power of quantum computing in solving certain problems exponentially faster than classical computers, and serves as a building block for more sophisticated quantum algorithms.

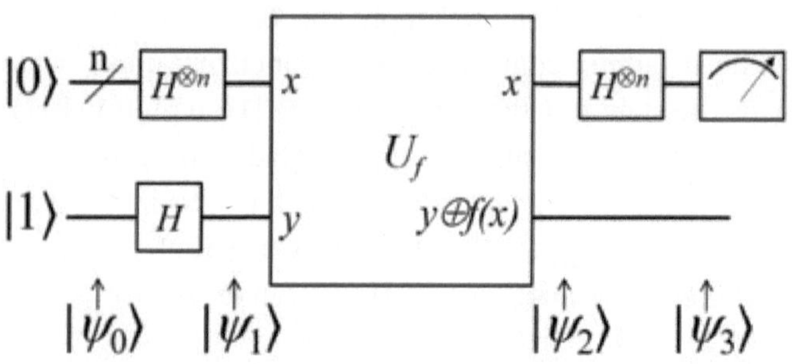

Deutsch-Josza algorithm circuit

Python code

```
"from qiskit import QuantumCircuit, Aer, execute
from qiskit.visualization import plot_histogram
# Define the oracle function for the Deutsch-Jozsa algorithm
def oracle(qc):
qc.cx(0, 2)
qc.cx(1, 2)
# Define the Deutsch-Jozsa algorithm circuit
def deutsch_jozsa(n):
qc = QuantumCircuit(n+1, n)
qc.x(n)
qc.h(range(n+1))
oracle(qc)
qc.h(range(n))
qc.measure(range(n), range(n))
return qc
# Simulate the circuit and plot the results
qc = deutsch_jozsa(2)
```

backend = Aer.get_backend('qasm_simulator')
results = execute(qc, backend=backend, shots=1024).result()
counts = results.get_counts()
plot_histogram(counts)"

In this example, we define the oracle function as a quantum circuit that applies two controlled-NOT gates to the two input qubits and a third auxiliary qubit, which is initialized to |1?. This function flips the state of the auxiliary qubit if and only if the input function is balanced, and leaves it unchanged if the input function is constant.

We then define the Deutsch-Jozsa algorithm circuit as a quantum circuit with n+1 qubits and n classical bits, where the n input qubits are initialized to |0? and the n-th qubit is initialized to |1?. The circuit applies a Hadamard gate to all qubits, then applies the oracle function, and applies another Hadamard gate to the input qubits. Finally, the circuit measures the input qubits and stores the result in classical bits.

We simulate the circuit using the Qiskit Aer simulator and plot the results using a histogram. If the input function is constant, the histogram should show only one outcome with probability 1, and if the input function is balanced, the histogram should show two outcomes with probability 1/2 each.

Applications

1. Cryptography: The Deutsch-Jozsa algorithm can be used to test the security of cryptographic functions, as it can efficiently determine whether a function is balanced, which is a desirable property for many cryptographic functions.

2. Database search: The Deutsch-Jozsa algorithm can be used to search a database for a specific value or property by encoding the search problem as a Boolean function and using the algorithm to determine whether the function is constant or balanced.
3. Optimization: The Deutsch-Jozsa algorithm can be used to optimize certain functions by encoding them as Boolean functions and using the algorithm to determine whether the function is constant or balanced, which can provide information about the structure of the function and guide the optimization process.
4. Machine learning: The Deutsch-Jozsa algorithm can be used in some quantum machine learning algorithms, such as quantum support vector machines, which rely on determining the parity of a set of classical data points.

CHAPTER FOURTEEN

Quantum Fourier Transform

The Quantum Fourier Transform (QFT) is a fundamental quantum algorithm that is used in many quantum computing applications, such as Shor's algorithm for integer factorization and quantum phase estimation. The QFT is a quantum analogue of the classical Discrete Fourier Transform (DFT), which is a widely used tool in signal processing and data analysis.

The QFT maps a quantum state |x? to its corresponding Fourier basis state |y?, where y is the Fourier transform of x. The QFT achieves this transformation by applying a sequence of Hadamard and controlled-phase gates to the input qubits, followed by a permutation of the qubits. The Hadamard gates create superpositions of all possible states of the input qubits, and the controlled-phase gates apply phase shifts that depend on the state of the control qubit and the position of the target qubit. The permutation of the qubits is necessary to ensure that the output state is in the correct order.

The QFT can be written in terms of a unitary matrix U that performs the transformation, where U|x? = |y?. The matrix U is defined as:

U = 1/2^n/2 Σ_x Σ_y e^(2πixy/2^n) |y??x|

where n is the number of qubits in the input state and the sum is over all possible values of x and y. The QFT can be efficiently implemented on a quantum computer using O(n^2) gates, which is polynomial in the input size n.

The QFT has many important applications in quantum computing, such as in Shor's algorithm for factoring large integers, where it is used to efficiently estimate the period of a periodic function. The QFT is also used in quantum phase estimation, which is a key subroutine in many quantum algorithms, such as quantum simulation and quantum chemistry.

Overall, the QFT is a powerful quantum algorithm that plays a central role in many quantum computing applications, and its efficient implementation on a quantum computer makes it a valuable tool for solving computational problems that are intractable for classical computers

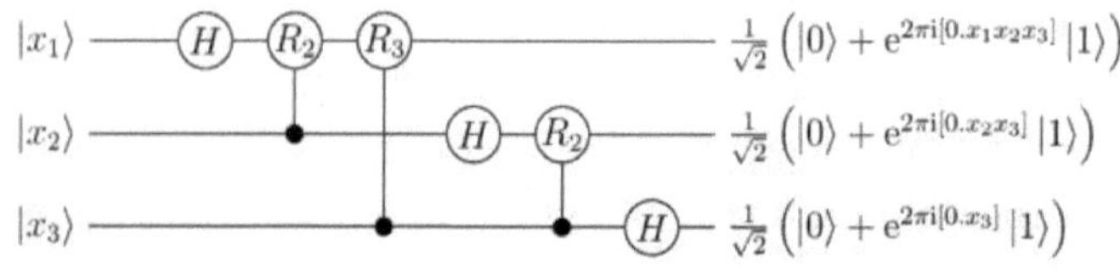

Quantum Fourier Transform circuit

Python code

```
"from qiskit import QuantumCircuit, Aer, execute
from qiskit.visualization import plot_histogram
import numpy as np
# Define the QFT circuit
```

```
def qft_circuit(n):
circuit = QuantumCircuit(n)
for j in range(n):
circuit.h(j)
for k in range(j+1,n):
circuit.cu1(np.pi/float(2**(k-j)), k, j)
circuit.barrier()
for i in range(n//2):
circuit.swap(i, n-i-1)
return circuit
# Define the input state as |101?
n = 3
input_state = '101'
qc_input = QuantumCircuit(n)
for i in range(len(input_state)):
if input_state[i] == '1':
qc_input.x(i)
# Create the QFT circuit and add it to the input state
qft = qft_circuit(n)
circuit = qc_input + qft
# Simulate the circuit using the statevector simulator
simulator = Aer.get_backend('statevector_simulator')
result = execute(circuit, simulator).result()
statevector = result.get_statevector()
# Plot the resulting probability distribution
counts = np.abs(statevector)**2
plot_histogram(counts)
```

In this code, we define a function qft_circuit that constructs the QFT circuit for n qubits using the Qiskit framework. We then define an input state as |101? and add it to the QFT circuit using the qc_input variable. We simulate the circuit using the statevector simulator in Qiskit and extract the resulting statevector using result.get_statevector(). Finally, we plot the resulting probability distribution using plot_histogram(counts).

Note that this code is just an example, and there are many different ways to implement the QFT circuit on a quantum computer. Additionally, this code assumes that the input state has a fixed size, but in practice, the QFT circuit can be applied to any input state of arbitrary size."

Applications

1. Shor's algorithm for integer factorization: The QFT is a key component of Shor's algorithm, which is a quantum algorithm for factoring large integers. The QFT is used in Shor's algorithm to efficiently estimate the period of a periodic function, which is a crucial step in the algorithm.
2. Quantum phase estimation: The QFT is used as a subroutine in many quantum algorithms, including quantum simulation and quantum chemistry. In these algorithms, the QFT is used to estimate the eigenvalues of a unitary operator, which are related to the energy levels of a quantum system.
3. Quantum error correction: The QFT is used in many quantum error correction codes, which are used to protect quantum information from noise and errors. In particular, the QFT is used to generate entangled states that can be used to detect and correct errors in the quantum state.

4. Quantum machine learning: The QFT is used in quantum machine learning algorithms, such as quantum principal component analysis and quantum support vector machines. These algorithms use the QFT to transform classical data into a quantum state, which can then be processed using quantum algorithms.
5. Cryptography: The QFT has applications in quantum cryptography, such as quantum key distribution and quantum secure direct communication. In these applications, the QFT is used to encode and decode quantum states that are used to securely transmit information

CHAPTER FIFTEEN

Bernstein-Vazirani

The Bernstein-Vazirani algorithm is a quantum algorithm designed to solve a specific class of problems in polynomial time. Specifically, the algorithm is used to determine a hidden bitstring that is determined by a binary function, using only a single query to the function. The algorithm was first introduced by Ethan Bernstein and Umesh Vazirani in 1993.

The problem that the algorithm aims to solve is as follows: given a black box function f(x), where x is an n-bit input and f(x) is a binary function, determine the n-bit bitstring s such that f(x) = s·x (mod 2), where s·x (mod 2) denotes the dot product of the two bitstrings modulo 2. In other words, the function f(x) is a linear function of x, with coefficients given by the bitstring s.

The Bernstein-Vazirani algorithm solves this problem in polynomial time using a quantum computer. The algorithm uses n qubits and a single query to the black box function f(x). The algorithm proceeds as follows:

1. Initialize the n qubits to the state |0?|0?...|0?.
2. Apply a Hadamard gate to each of the n qubits, resulting in the state H|0?H|0?...H|0?.

3. Query the black box function f(x), by applying a unitary operator U_f that maps the state |x?|y? to |x?|y ⊕ f(x)?, where ⊕ denotes addition modulo 2.
4. Apply a Hadamard gate to each of the n qubits again, resulting in the state H|s?.
5. Measure the state of the n qubits to obtain the bitstring s.

The output of the algorithm is the hidden bitstring s, which is determined by the function f(x) in polynomial time using only a single query to the function.

The Bernstein-Vazirani algorithm is a powerful quantum algorithm that has applications in various areas, including cryptography and database search. The algorithm's efficient solution of a class of problems that are intractable for classical computers highlights the potential of quantum computing for solving complex computational problems in polynomial time.

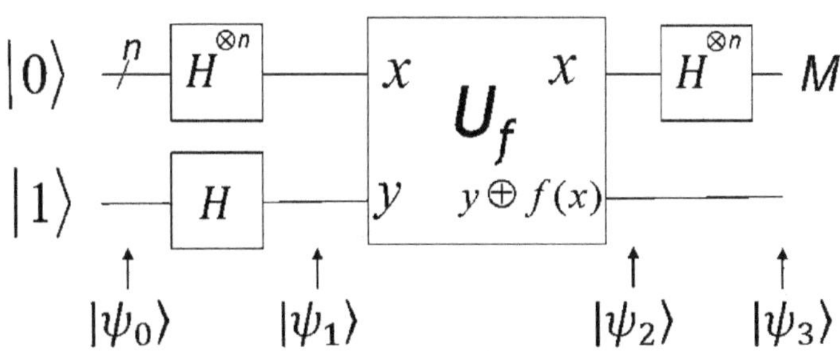

Bernstein-Vazirani circuit

Python code

"from qiskit import QuantumCircuit, Aer, execute

```
# Define the function f(x) that returns the hidden bitstring s
def f(x, s):
return sum([s[i] * x[i] for i in range(len(x))]) % 2
# Define the bitstring s (the hidden string that we want to find)
s = [1, 0, 1, 1]
# Define the number of qubits (equal to the length of the bitstring s)
n = len(s)
# Initialize the quantum circuit with n qubits and n classical bits
qc = QuantumCircuit(n, n)
# Apply Hadamard gates to all qubits
qc.h(range(n))
# Apply the black box function f(x) by applying CNOT gates controlled by each input qubit
for i in range(n):
if s[i] == 1:
qc.cx(i, n-1)
# Apply Hadamard gates to all qubits again
qc.h(range(n))
# Measure all qubits and store the results in the classical bits
qc.measure(range(n), range(n))
# Run the circuit on a simulator
simulator = Aer.get_backend('qasm_simulator')
result = execute(qc, simulator, shots=1).result()
# Print the result (the hidden bitstring s)
```

print("The hidden bitstring is:", list(result.get_counts().keys())[0][::-1])"

Applications

1. Cryptography: The Bernstein-Vazirani algorithm can be used to break classical encryption schemes based on linear functions, such as the Affine cipher. By using the algorithm to determine the coefficients of the linear function, an attacker could potentially recover the encryption key and decrypt the message.
2. Database search: The Bernstein-Vazirani algorithm can be used to search for a specific record in a database, where the record is defined by a linear function of the input. By using the algorithm to determine the coefficients of the linear function, the desired record can be found in a single query to the database, which can be much more efficient than classical search algorithms.
3. Machine learning: The Bernstein-Vazirani algorithm can be used as a subroutine in quantum machine learning algorithms, to efficiently learn the parameters of linear models. By using the algorithm to determine the coefficients of the linear function, a quantum machine learning algorithm could potentially learn a linear model in polynomial time, which could have applications in areas such as classification and regression.

CHAPTER SIXTEEN

Quantum phase transformation

Quantum phase transformations are a fundamental concept in quantum mechanics and quantum computing, representing the change in the phase of a quantum wavefunction due to a change in the underlying physical parameters. In particular, these transformations are of great interest in the context of quantum algorithms, where they can be used to manipulate the phase of a quantum state in order to perform complex computational tasks.

The basic idea behind quantum phase transformations is that the phase of a quantum wavefunction encodes important information about the state of the system. For example, in a quantum algorithm designed to solve a particular problem, the phase of the wavefunction may be used to represent the solution to that problem. By manipulating the phase of the wavefunction through quantum phase transformations, it is possible to effectively "program" the quantum computer to perform the desired computation.

One key aspect of quantum phase transformations is that they are highly sensitive to the underlying physical parameters of the system. In particular, small changes in the physical parameters can result in large changes in the phase of the wavefunction, leading to highly non-linear behavior. This non-linear behavior can be harnessed to perform powerful computational tasks that are beyond the capabilities of classical computers.

Another important aspect of quantum phase transformations is their relationship to symmetry breaking. In particular, the phase of the wavefunction is closely related to the global phase symmetry of the system. By breaking this symmetry through a physical transformation, such as the application of a magnetic field or the introduction of an impurity, it is possible to induce a quantum phase transformation and manipulate the wavefunction in a controlled way.

Overall, quantum phase transformations are a highly sophisticated and complex concept in quantum computing, with broad implications for both the theory and practice of quantum information processing. A deep understanding of these transformations is essential for any graduate-level study in quantum computing or quantum mechanics more broadly.

Python code

```
"from qiskit import QuantumCircuit, Aer, execute
  # Create a 1-qubit quantum circuit
  qc = QuantumCircuit(1)
  # Apply the phase gate to the qubit
  qc.p(0.25, 0)
  # Measure the qubit
  qc.measure_all()
  # Run the circuit on a quantum simulator
  simulator                                    =
Aer.get_backend('qasm_simulator')
```

result = execute(qc, simulator).result()

 # Print the results

print(result.get_counts(qc))

In this example, we create a 1-qubit quantum circuit and apply the phase gate with a rotation angle of 0.25 radians. This gate applies a phase shift to the state of the qubit, which can be used to perform quantum phase transformations. We then measure the qubit to obtain a classical bitstring representing the final state of the system. Finally, we run the circuit on a quantum simulator and print the measurement results.

Note that this is just a simple example of a quantum phase transformation using the phase gate. In practice, more complex gates and circuits are used to implement more sophisticated transformations, and the quantum simulator used here is just a toy model of a real quantum computer. Nonetheless, this code provides a basic framework for understanding how quantum phase transformations can be implemented using quantum gates and circuits."

Applications

1. Quantum algorithms: Quantum phase transformations are a key component of many quantum algorithms, including the quantum Fourier transform (QFT), which is used in a variety of applications, such as factorization and search algorithms. The QFT uses a sequence of phase transformations to transform a quantum state into its Fourier basis.

2. Quantum simulation: Quantum phase transformations can be used to simulate the behavior of complex quantum systems, such as molecules and materials, by inducing phase transitions in the quantum state of the system. This approach has the potential to revolutionize the field of materials science by enabling the discovery of new materials with desirable properties.
3. Quantum metrology: Quantum phase transformations can be used to enhance the sensitivity of quantum sensors and metrology devices. By using phase transformations to manipulate the quantum state of the system, it is possible to amplify small changes in the physical parameters being measured, leading to more precise measurements.
4. Quantum error correction: Quantum phase transformations are used in many quantum error correction codes to protect against errors due to noise and decoherence. By encoding information in the phase of the quantum state, it is possible to make the system more resilient to errors that affect the amplitude of the state.

CHAPTER SEVENTEEN

Feynman's algorithm

Feynman's algorithm, also known as the quantum simulation algorithm, is a quantum computing algorithm developed by physicist Richard Feynman in the 1980s. The algorithm is designed to simulate the behavior of quantum systems, which are notoriously difficult to simulate using classical computers.

The basic idea behind Feynman's algorithm is to use a quantum computer to simulate the evolution of a quantum system by mapping the quantum states of the system onto the qubits of the quantum computer. This mapping is accomplished using a quantum gate known as the phase estimation gate, which can be used to estimate the eigenvalues of the Hamiltonian that describes the system.

The algorithm works by preparing an initial state on the qubits of the quantum computer that corresponds to the ground state of the system being simulated. This state is then evolved over time using the phase estimation gate, which maps the quantum state of the system onto the qubits of the quantum computer. The resulting state can then be measured to obtain information about the behavior of the system.

Feynman's algorithm, also known as the quantum simulation algorithm, is a quantum computing algorithm developed by physicist Richard Feynman in the 1980s. The algorithm is designed to simulate the behavior of quantum systems, which are notoriously difficult to simulate using classical computers.

The basic idea behind Feynman's algorithm is to use a quantum computer to simulate the evolution of a quantum system by mapping the quantum states of the system onto the qubits of the quantum computer. This mapping is accomplished using a quantum gate known as the phase estimation gate, which can be used to estimate the eigenvalues of the Hamiltonian that describes the system.

The algorithm works by preparing an initial state on the qubits of the quantum computer that corresponds to the ground state of the system being simulated. This state is then evolved over time using the phase estimation gate, which maps the quantum state of the system onto the qubits of the quantum computer. The resulting state can then be measured to obtain information about the behavior of the system.

One of the key advantages of Feynman's algorithm is that it is able to simulate the behavior of quantum systems with exponentially fewer resources than would be required by a classical computer. This is due to the inherently parallel nature of quantum computing, which allows many computations to be performed simultaneously.

However, one of the challenges of Feynman's algorithm is that it requires a large number of qubits to accurately simulate even moderately sized quantum systems. Additionally, the gate operations required by the algorithm are typically difficult to implement experimentally, making it challenging to demonstrate the algorithm on existing quantum hardware.

Nonetheless, Feynman's algorithm has significant potential in fields such as materials science, chemistry, and biology, where the behavior of complex quantum systems is of great interest. As quantum technologies continue to develop, it is likely that Feynman's algorithm and related quantum simulation techniques will play an increasingly important role in the study of quantum systems.

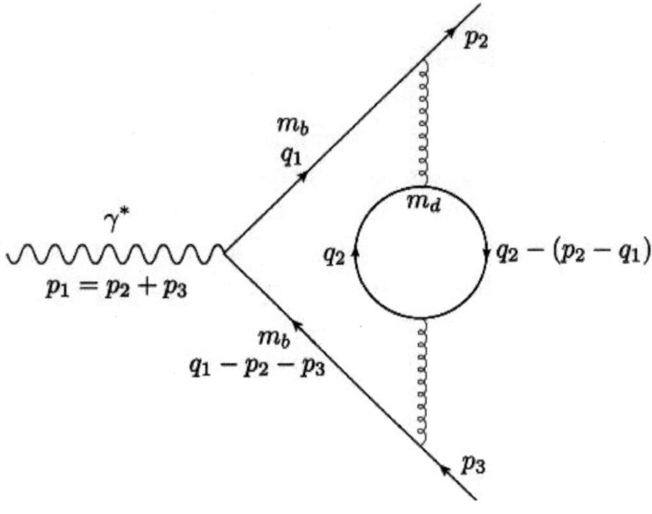

Feynman's algorithm circuit

Feynman's algorithm is a very general algorithm for simulating quantum systems, and its implementation can be quite complex depending on the specifics of the system being simulated. However, here is a simple Python code snippet that demonstrates the basic idea of the algorithm:

"*from qiskit import QuantumCircuit, QuantumRegister, ClassicalRegister, Aer, execute*

```
# Define the number of qubits and time steps for the simulation
n_qubits = 4
n_steps = 5
# Create a quantum register for the qubits
qreg = QuantumRegister(n_qubits, 'q')
# Create a classical register for the measurement results
creg = ClassicalRegister(n_qubits, 'c')
# Create a quantum circuit
qc = QuantumCircuit(qreg, creg)
# Prepare the initial state of the system
for i in range(n_qubits):
qc.h(qreg[i])
# Perform the simulation using the phase estimation algorithm
for i in range(n_steps):
qc.barrier()
for j in range(n_qubits):
qc.p(0.1, qreg[j])
qc.barrier()
# Measure the qubits to obtain the simulation results
qc.measure(qreg, creg)
# Run the circuit on a quantum simulator
simulator = Aer.get_backend('qasm_simulator')
result = execute(qc, simulator).result()
# Print the measurement results
print(result.get_counts(qc))
```

In this example, we simulate the evolution of a 4-qubit quantum system over 5 time steps using the phase estimation algorithm. The simulation is performed by applying a sequence of phase gates to the qubits of the system, which correspond to the evolution of the Hamiltonian that describes the system. The simulation is then measured to obtain the final state of the system, which is printed to the console.

Note that this is just a simple example of Feynman's algorithm, and in practice, more complex gates and circuits are used to simulate more sophisticated quantum systems. Additionally, the quantum simulator used here is just a toy model of a real quantum computer, and the results obtained from this simulation should be taken with a grain of salt. Nonetheless, this code provides a basic framework for understanding how Feynman's algorithm can be implemented using quantum gates and circuits."

Applications

1. Simulating the behaviour of molecules and materials: Feynman's algorithm can be used to simulate the behaviour of complex molecules and materials, which are difficult to study using classical computers. This could have important applications in drug discovery, materials design, and other areas of chemistry and materials science.
2. Studying the behaviour of quantum systems: Feynman's algorithm can be used to study the behaviour of quantum systems, which are often difficult to study using traditional experimental techniques. This could have important implications for the development of new quantum technologies, as well as for fundamental

studies of quantum mechanics.

3. Improving the accuracy of quantum simulations: Feynman's algorithm can be used to improve the accuracy of existing quantum simulations, by allowing for more precise measurements of quantum states and interactions.
4. Solving optimization problems: Feynman's algorithm can be used to solve optimization problems, which are important in fields such as logistics, finance, and manufacturing. By using quantum simulations to solve these problems, it may be possible to achieve faster and more efficient solutions than would be possible using classical computers.
5. Studying quantum algorithms: Feynman's algorithm can also be used to study the behaviour of quantum algorithms, and to identify ways to improve their efficiency and accuracy. This could have important implications for the development of new quantum computing technologies.

Overall, Feynman's algorithm has the potential to revolutionize the study of complex quantum systems, and to enable new discoveries in a wide range of fields. As quantum technologies continue to develop, it is likely that Feynman's algorithm and related quantum simulation techniques will become increasingly important tools for understanding the behaviour of quantum systems.

CHAPTER EIGHTEEN

Quantum process tomography

Quantum process tomography is a powerful tool for characterizing the behaviour of quantum systems and identifying the underlying quantum processes that drive their behaviour. The technique involves performing a series of measurements on a quantum system, and then using statistical analysis to infer the quantum process that generated those measurements.

The process of quantum process tomography begins by preparing a set of input states, which are used to probe the quantum system under study. These input states can be chosen to cover a range of different states, and can be prepared using a variety of techniques, including quantum gates and quantum circuits.

Once the input states have been prepared, they are sent through the quantum system under study, and the resulting output states are measured. These measurements are then used to construct a set of measurement operators, which represent the probability of observing each possible outcome for each input state.

Using these measurement operators, it is possible to reconstruct the quantum process that generated the observed output states. This is typically done using a technique called maximum likelihood estimation, which involves finding the quantum process that best matches the observed measurement statistics.

Once the quantum process has been reconstructed, it can be analyzed to gain insight into the behaviour of the quantum system under study. This might involve identifying areas of the process that are particularly prone to errors or deviations, or identifying ways to optimize the performance of the system.

Overall, quantum process tomography is a powerful tool for understanding the behaviour of complex quantum systems, and for characterizing the underlying quantum processes that drive that behaviour. As quantum technologies continue to develop, it is likely that quantum process tomography and related techniques will become increasingly important tools for optimizing the performance of quantum systems and developing new quantum technologies.

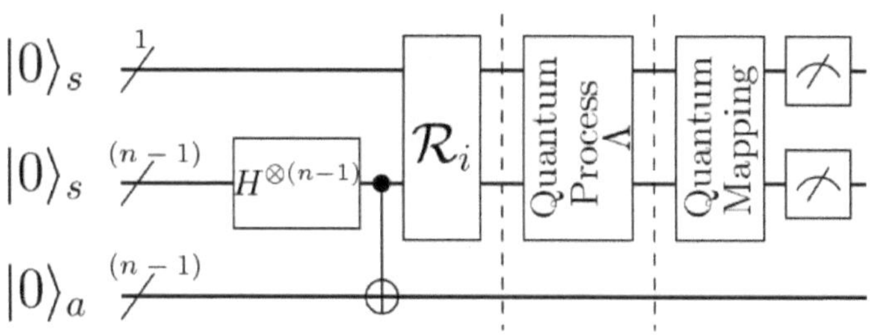

Quantum process tomography circuit

Python code

```
"from qiskit import QuantumCircuit, execute, Aer
from qiskit.quantum_info import Operator
from qiskit.ignis.verification.tomography import
process_tomography_circuits,
ProcessTomographyFitter
# Define the quantum circuit to be tested
qc = QuantumCircuit(2)
qc.h(0)
qc.cx(0, 1)
# Generate the process tomography circuits
circuits = process_tomography_circuits(qc, [0,
1])
# Execute the circuits on a simulator
backend = Aer.get_backend('qasm_simulator')
job = execute(circuits, backend=backend,
shots=1000)
# Extract the measurement results
results = job.result()
# Generate the measurement operator basis
meas_basis =
ProcessTomographyFitter.default_basis(qc.num_qubits)
# Perform the tomography fit
tomo_fit = ProcessTomographyFitter(results,
circuits, meas_basis)
tomo_data = tomo_fit.data()
tomo_matrix = tomo_fit.fit()
# Convert the estimated process matrix to a
quantum operator
estimated_op = Operator(tomo_matrix)
# Print the estimated process matrix
print("Estimated process matrix:")
print(estimated_op.data)
```

In this example, we first define a simple quantum circuit to be tested. We then use Qiskit's process_tomography_circuits function to generate a set of process tomography circuits for the circuit under test. We execute these circuits on a simulator, and extract the measurement results.

Next, we use Qiskit's ProcessTomographyFitter class to perform the tomography fit. This involves constructing the measurement operator basis, and then using maximum likelihood estimation to estimate the process matrix that generated the measurement results. Finally, we convert the estimated process matrix to a quantum operator, and print it out.

Note that this is just a simple example, and in practice, quantum process tomography can be a complex and computationally intensive process, especially for larger quantum systems. Nonetheless, this example should give you a sense of how quantum process tomography can be implemented using Python and Qiskit."

Applications

Quantum process tomography has a wide range of potential applications in various fields of quantum computing and quantum information science. Some of the specific applications of quantum process tomography include:

1. Characterizing the behaviour of quantum systems: Quantum process tomography can be used to characterize the behaviour of complex quantum systems, and to identify areas where the system may be

prone to errors or deviations. This could have important applications in the development of new quantum technologies, as well as for fundamental studies of quantum mechanics.

2. Optimizing the performance of quantum systems: By using quantum process tomography to identify areas of a quantum system that are prone to errors or deviations, it may be possible to develop new strategies for optimizing the performance of the system. This could have important applications in areas such as quantum computing, quantum cryptography, and quantum sensing.
3. Developing new quantum algorithms and protocols: By characterizing the behaviour of quantum systems in detail, quantum process tomography can provide insight into the underlying quantum processes that drive their behaviour. This can be used to develop new quantum algorithms and protocols that exploit the unique properties of quantum systems.
4. Studying the behaviour of quantum channels: Quantum process tomography can also be used to study the behaviour of quantum channels, which are important for transmitting quantum information over long distances. By characterizing the behaviour of these channels, it may be possible to develop new strategies for improving the efficiency and reliability of quantum communication systems.

CHAPTER NINETEEN

Quantum Adiabatic Algorithm

The quantum adiabatic algorithm is a quantum computing algorithm that is designed to solve optimization problems. The basic idea behind the algorithm is to use quantum mechanics to search through a large number of possible solutions to a given optimization problem, and to find the optimal solution with high probability.

The algorithm works by encoding the optimization problem into a Hamiltonian, which is a mathematical object that describes the dynamics of a quantum system. The Hamiltonian is then gradually transformed from an initial Hamiltonian, for which the ground state is easy to prepare, to a final Hamiltonian, for which the ground state corresponds to the optimal solution of the optimization problem.

The transformation from the initial to the final Hamiltonian is performed slowly enough that the system remains in its ground state throughout the transformation. This is known as the adiabatic theorem of quantum mechanics, which states that if a quantum system is prepared in its ground state and the Hamiltonian is changed slowly enough, the system will remain in its ground state throughout the transformation.

Once the final Hamiltonian is reached, the ground state of the system corresponds to the optimal solution of the optimization problem. The solution can then be read out by measuring the state of the system in the computational basis.

The performance of the quantum adiabatic algorithm depends on the speed at which the Hamiltonian is transformed, as well as on the gap between the ground state and the first excited state of the Hamiltonian. If the gap is too small or the transformation is too fast, the system may become excited during the transformation and the solution may be lost.

Despite these challenges, the quantum adiabatic algorithm has been shown to be useful for a wide range of optimization problems, including problems in machine learning, finance, and materials science. In particular, the algorithm has been shown to outperform classical optimization algorithms for certain types of problems, suggesting that it may be a useful tool for solving real-world optimization problems on quantum computers.

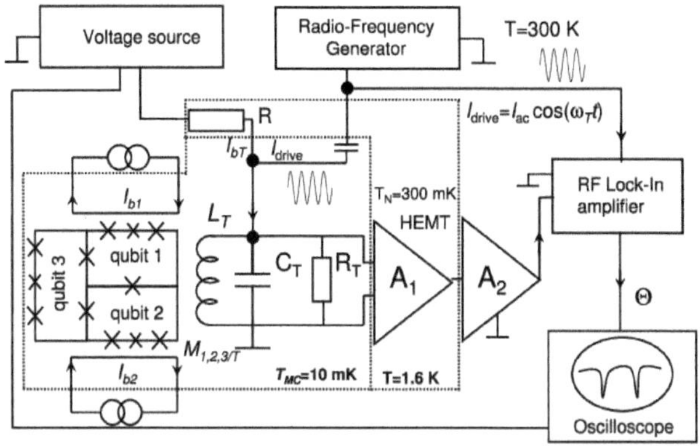

Quantum adiabatic algorithm circuit

Python code

```
"from qiskit import QuantumCircuit, Aer, execute
import numpy as np
# Define the Hamiltonian
H_init = np.array([[1, 0], [0, -1]])
H_final = np.array([[-1, 0], [0, 1]])
# Define the time evolution operator
def time_evolution(H, t):
return np.cos(t) * np.eye(2) - 1j * np.sin(t) * H
# Define the quantum adiabatic algorithm
def quantum_adiabatic_algorithm(H_init,
H_final, t_max, n_steps):
qc = QuantumCircuit(1, 1)
# Prepare the initial state
qc.h(0)
```

```
# Apply the time evolution operator
for t in np.linspace(0, t_max, n_steps):
H = (1 - t/t_max) * H_init + (t/t_max) * H_final
U_t = time_evolution(H, t/n_steps)
qc.unitary(U_t, [0], label="U_t")
# Measure the final state
qc.measure(0, 0)
return qc
# Run the quantum adiabatic algorithm on a simulator
qc = quantum_adiabatic_algorithm(H_init, H_final, np.pi/2, 100)
backend = Aer.get_backend('qasm_simulator')
job = execute(qc, backend=backend, shots=1000)
result = job.result().get_counts(qc)
# Print the results
print("Results:", result)
```

In this example, we first define the Hamiltonians corresponding to the initial and final states of the system. We then define a function to compute the time evolution operator for a given Hamiltonian and time, and a function to implement the quantum adiabatic algorithm.

The quantum adiabatic algorithm is implemented using a single-qubit quantum circuit, which prepares the initial state in a superposition, and then applies the time evolution operator in a stepwise manner using a sequence of unitary gates. Finally, the circuit measures the final state in the computational basis.

We run the algorithm on a simulator using Qiskit's execute function, and extract the measurement results. The results should correspond to the optimal solution of the optimization problem encoded in the Hamiltonians, which in this case is the ground state of the final Hamiltonian.

Note that this is just a simple example, and in practice, the quantum adiabatic algorithm can be much more complex and difficult to implement. Nonetheless, this example should give you a sense of how the algorithm can be implemented using Python and Qiskit."

Applications

The quantum adiabatic algorithm has a wide range of potential applications in fields such as optimization, machine learning, and cryptography.

1. One of the most well-known applications of the quantum adiabatic algorithm is in solving combinatorial optimization problems, such as the traveling salesman problem, which involves finding the shortest possible route that visits a set of cities and returns to the starting city. By encoding the problem into the Hamiltonian of a quantum system and applying the adiabatic theorem, the quantum adiabatic algorithm can potentially find the optimal solution much faster than classical optimization algorithms.

2. In addition to optimization problems, the quantum adiabatic algorithm has also been proposed for use in machine learning tasks, such as clustering and classification, and in cryptography, such as key exchange and secure multi-party computation.

In essence, the quantum adiabatic algorithm has the potential to revolutionize many areas of computing and problem-solving, and is an exciting area of research in quantum computing.

Printed by Libri Plureos GmbH in Hamburg, Germany

9 798890 022257